AI FOR SMALL BUSINESS OWNERS

A Practical Guide to Robotics,

Automation, and Sustainable Growth

CONTENTS

CHAPTER 1

•———————————•

WHAT IS AI, REALLY?

Introduction

Artificial Intelligence (AI) is no longer a futuristic concept, it's a working part of modern business. What used to be reserved for tech giants is now embedded in everyday tools that any business owner can access.

From automating responses to writing blog posts and analyzing customer data, AI is becoming a quiet workhorse behind the scenes of many small and midsize companies. But while AI's power is increasing, many small business owners still ask the same first question:

What exactly is AI—and what can it really do for me?

This chapter will answer that question in plain English. No hype. No buzzwords. Just clear explanations of what AI is, how it works, and why it matters to your business.

What Artificial Intelligence Actually Means

At its core, **artificial intelligence** is about getting machines to perform tasks that would normally require human intelligence. That includes things like:

- Understanding and generating language

- Recognizing patterns and trends

- Making predictions

- Learning from data

- Solving problems or responding to input

In practical terms, AI is just very smart software. It can be used to:

- Write content for websites, emails, and ads

- Respond to customer messages automatically

- Analyze large sets of data to find useful insights

- Organize schedules or automate workflow tasks

- Recommend products, prices, or next steps

AI doesn't think or feel—it analyzes and calculates based on training and data. Its strength lies in how fast it can process huge amounts of information and generate results.

You're Probably Already Using AI

Even if you don't realize it, you're likely already using AI in your business or personal life:

- Your email app filters spam and suggests responses.

- Google Maps adjusts your route in real time.

- Netflix and Spotify recommend content based on your preferences.

- Online stores suggest products you may like.

- Voice assistants respond to natural language commands.

These are examples of **narrow AI**—systems trained to perform specific tasks. The tools discussed in this book use the same core principles and models but apply them directly to business tasks like content creation, scheduling, automation, and decision-making.

Key Concepts You Should Understand

1. Artificial Intelligence (AI)

A broad term referring to machines or software systems designed to simulate aspects of human intelligence. These systems can interpret information, learn patterns, and make decisions.

2. Machine Learning (ML)

A method used to train AI systems by feeding them large amounts of data so they can learn and improve over time. For example, a system might learn to recognize spam emails by analyzing thousands of examples.

3. Natural Language Processing (NLP)

The ability of AI to understand and respond to human language. This is the technology behind tools like ChatGPT, customer support bots, and voice assistants.

4. Large Language Models (LLMs)

A type of AI model trained in massive amounts of text to generate human-like writing, respond to prompts, and carry on conversations. ChatGPT is an example of an LLM.

5. Automation

Software that performs tasks without manual input. While not all automation uses AI, many modern automation tools include AI to help handle more complex tasks intelligently.

What AI Is Not

To be clear, AI is not:

- A human-like robot that can think independently
- A replacement for strategic thinking or emotional intelligence
- Capable of replacing your entire business team

It also doesn't work miracles. AI needs clear input, realistic goals, and human oversight to be useful. It's a tool—not a magic wand.

Why AI Is a Big Deal for Small Businesses

If you're running a small business, you're likely managing dozens of responsibilities with limited time, staff, and budget. That's exactly where AI can give you an advantage.

Here's why AI is especially valuable for small business owners:

- **It saves time.** AI can handle repetitive tasks like scheduling, content creation, or customer replies—freeing you up to focus on growth.

- **It improves output.** AI tools can help you write faster, design better visuals, and analyze data more efficiently.

- **It's affordable.** Many powerful AI tools now offer free or low-cost plans designed for individuals and small teams.

- **It boosts consistency.** Automated responses, AI-generated content, and repeatable workflows mean fewer missed steps or forgotten tasks.

- **It helps you compete.** With the right tools, you can look, sound, and operate like a much larger organization.

In other words, AI doesn't just make work faster, it can also make your business more professional, consistent, and scalable.

A Real-World Business Example

Let's say you run a boutique consulting firm. You're juggling client onboarding, marketing, proposals, invoicing, and follow-ups.

Here's how AI can step in:

- Use **ChatGPT** to write proposals and email responses.

- Use **Canva AI** to create branded content for social media.

- Use **Zapier** to automate client onboarding steps (form → email → calendar invite).

- Use **Fireflies.ai** to automatically record and summarize client calls.

- Use **Copy.ai** to generate weekly LinkedIn posts promoting your services.

Result? You reclaim 8–10 hours per week. Your brand becomes more consistent. Your clients experience faster, more professional communication—and you get to focus on strategic work instead of repeating the same manual tasks.

Tools to Know (As of April 2025)

Tool	Purpose	Free Version	Paid Plan
ChatGPT	Writing and content generation	Yes	$20/month (GPT-4)
Canva AI	Design and social visuals	Yes	$12.99/month (Pro)
Zapier	Workflow automation	Yes	From $0 to $49/month
Copy.ai	Short-form marketing copy	Yes	$36/month (Pro)
Fireflies.ai	Meeting transcription and summaries	Yes	$10/month (Pro)

All tools listed here were verified and up to date as of April 2025. Pricing may vary. Always check the provider's official site before committing.

Summary

AI isn't some abstract concept anymore. It's a real, practical toolkit you can use right now. Whether you're looking to improve your content, automate routine tasks, or gain insights from your data, AI offers powerful options—often at low cost and with minimal setup.

In the next chapter, you'll learn **why AI matters so much, specifically for small businesses**, and how adopting it early can help you stay ahead in a fast-changing world.

CHAPTER 2

•————————————•

WHY AI MATTERS FOR SMALL BUSINESSES

Introduction

For small business owners, time is your most limited asset. You're balancing sales, marketing, admin, service delivery, and often doing it with a small team—or no team at all.

That's where AI becomes not just helpful, but essential. It offers a rare opportunity to **work smarter, not harder**, allowing you to operate with the power and polish of a much larger company— without the overhead.

This chapter explains why AI is especially important for small business success and how it helps you win in a competitive market.

What Makes Small Businesses Unique

Running a small business often means:

- Limited staff and time

- Tight budgets

- A need to handle many roles yourself

- Competing against larger, better-funded competitors

These constraints demand efficiency, agility, and tools that can scale with you as you grow. AI meets these demands by acting like a digital assistant that works 24/7, doesn't take breaks, and costs less than hiring extra staff.

Five Reasons AI Gives You a Competitive Edge

1. AI Saves Time

Most business owners spend hours on repetitive work:

- Answering the same customer questions

- Writing social media captions

- Following up with leads

- Organizing schedules or meetings

AI can do most of this **automatically**, saving hours each week and letting you focus on tasks that need your expertise.

2. AI Reduces Cost

Hiring help is expensive. But with the right AI tools:

- You don't need a full-time assistant to manage your inbox.

- You don't need a copywriter to produce content.

- You don't need a social media manager to schedule posts.

AI gives you **specialist-level capability** for a fraction of the cost.

3. AI Increases Consistency

When you're managing a dozen things at once, consistency can slip. AI helps standardize your:

- Branding

- Messaging

- Responses

- Service quality

It makes sure your business sounds and feels the same—every time, on every channel.

4. AI Enhances Customer Experience

AI can personalize emails, recommend content, and even reply instantly to common customer questions. This creates a faster, smoother experience that keeps customers coming back.

5. AI Helps You Scale

As your business grows, AI systems can grow with you. Automations can be duplicated, content generation can be expanded, and customer data can be managed more intelligently.

AI gives you the infrastructure to handle more clients or customers—without burning out.

Real Business Use Cases

Example 1: Solo Service Provider

A consultant uses AI to:

- Write newsletters with ChatGPT

- Automate appointment scheduling with Calendly

- Summarize calls using Fireflies.ai
  Outcome: 10 hours per week saved

Example 2: Product-Based Business

A retailer uses AI to:

- Generate product descriptions with Copy.ai

- Create ad graphics with Canva AI

- Schedule social posts automatically
  Outcome: Doubled marketing output with zero additional staff

Example 3: Local Business

A yoga studio uses AI to:

- Manage customer check-ins with QR codes

- Send automatic reminders

- Collect reviews using smart forms

  Outcome: Improved client engagement and reduced no-shows

What Happens If You Wait?

Many business owners say, "I'll try AI later." But delaying AI adoption means:

- Missing out on cost savings and time

- Falling behind competitors who are already using it

- Making future systems upgrades harder as old habits become ingrained

The best time to start using AI is now—even if you start small.

Recommended Tools to Explore (As of April 2025)

Tool	Use Case	Free Version	Paid Plan
ChatGPT	Writing and content	Yes	$20/month (GPT-4)
Grammarly	Writing improvement	Yes	$12/month
Copy.ai	Product and ad copy	Yes	$36/month
Calendly	Scheduling and automation	Yes	From $10/month
Fireflies.ai	Meeting transcription	Yes	$10/month (Pro)

Summary

AI isn't just a nice-to-have. It's quickly becoming a **business advantage**, especially for small businesses that need to do more with less resources. By reducing your workload, improving your customer experience, and helping you compete on a bigger stage, AI becomes a trusted partner in your business.

In the next chapter, we'll explain **what AI is made of**—the technology behind the scenes—so you can make smart decisions without needing to be a tech expert.

CHAPTER 3

WHAT AI IS MADE OF (WITHOUT MAKING YOUR BRAIN HURT)

Introduction

To use AI well, you don't need to become a software engineer. But you *do* need a working understanding of what AI is made of, how it functions, and what's happening behind the curtain.

That way, you can make better decisions about:

- Which tools to trust

- What features are worth paying for

- Where AI adds real value—and where it doesn't

This chapter explains AI's core components in a clear, approachable way.

The Five Core Ingredients of AI

1. Data

Data is the raw material AI learns from. It includes:

- Written content (books, websites, emails)

- Images and videos

- Numbers (sales data, customer activity)

- Audio or speech transcripts

The more relevant, accurate data an AI system has access to, the better its output.

2. Models

A model is a trained system that processes data to produce results. Models are built to recognize patterns and generate predictions or content based on what they've learned.

Some models specialize in language (like ChatGPT), while others are built for visuals, forecasting, or voice recognition.

3. Training

Training is how models learn. During training:

- AI is fed large datasets (millions or billions of examples)

- It starts recognizing relationships, similarities, and patterns

- The model improves over time with more exposure and adjustments

You don't need to train models yourself—most business tools come pre-trained—but it helps to know that better training usually means better performance.

4. Algorithms

Algorithms are the rules the AI follows to analyze input and deliver output. Think of them as recipes that guide what the model does with the data it's given.

Different AI tools use different algorithms, which is why some are better at language, others at images, and others at recommendations or forecasts.

5. Interfaces

The interface is what you interact with: the website, app, or platform that lets you enter a prompt, upload content, or click a button to run the AI.

A great interface makes a powerful model easy to use, which is why even complex systems like ChatGPT feel accessible to non-technical users.

Understanding Tool Types

There are three main categories of AI tools you'll encounter:

- **No-Code Tools**
  Built for non-technical users. You click, type, and use

templates.

Examples: ChatGPT, Canva AI, Jasper

- **Low-Code Tools**

  Requires some setup or configuration, but no advanced coding.

  Examples: Zapier, Make (formerly Integromat)

- **Full-Code Tools**

  Built for developers and engineers.

  Examples: OpenAI API, custom Python models

For small businesses, **no-code and low-code tools** are ideal. They're affordable, easy to learn, and fast to implement.

Tool Examples by Capability (As of April 2025)

Business Task	Tool Example	AI Function
Write content	ChatGPT, Jasper	Language model (LLM)
Generate graphics	Canva AI, Firefly	Generative image AI
Automate workflows	Zapier, Make	Rule-based + smart triggers
Analyze customer behavior	Zoho Analytics, Looker Studio	Predictive analysis

What Makes One Tool "Smarter" Than Another?

Not all AI tools are equal. What separates great tools from average ones?

- Quality of training data

- Strength of the model (GPT-4 vs older models)

- User interface design

- How well it adapts or customizes to your brand or needs

When evaluating a new tool, ask:

- Does it consistently produce quality output?

- Does it learn or improve based on your usage?

- Is it flexible enough to adapt to your workflow?

Summary

AI may seem complex under the hood, but as a business owner, you only need to understand a few key ideas to use it well. With that foundation, you're ready to evaluate tools, make smart investments, and integrate AI more confidently into your business.

In the next chapter, we'll dive into how to **choose the right tools** for your specific business—without wasting time or money.

CHAPTER 4

•————————————•

CHOOSING THE RIGHT AI TOOLS FOR YOUR BUSINESS

Introduction

The market is flooded with AI tools. New apps appear weekly, all promising to save time, boost productivity, or revolutionize your business. But not every tool is worth your time—or your money.

This chapter will help you avoid shiny object syndrome by showing you how to **choose tools based on real business needs**, not trends. You'll learn how to evaluate AI platforms the way a strategist would: with clarity, practicality, and focus.

Step 1: Identify the Business Task

Before searching for any tool, ask:
"What problem do I want to solve?"

Start with real tasks that are slowing you down or limiting your growth.

Examples:

- Writing blog posts takes too long

- Leads are falling through the cracks

- You forget to follow up with prospects

- Social media posts are inconsistent

AI works best when you apply it to a **specific, repeatable task** that you currently handle manually.

Step 2: Match the Task to a Tool Type

Now match your need to a general category of tool:

Business Need	Tool Type
Write content	Language models (LLMs)
Create images or videos	Generative AI
Automate workflows	Automation tools
Schedule meetings or follow-ups	Calendar + task automation
Analyze customer or sales data	AI-driven analytics

This ensures you don't end up using a design tool when you really need help with organization—or a chatbot when you need a scheduler.

Step 3: Choose the Simplest Tool That Works

For small businesses, the best AI tools are:

- Easy to learn

- Quick to set up

- Compatible with tools you already use

- Built for non-technical users

Don't fall for platforms that look powerful but require technical skills you don't have. **Start simple**, and upgrade later if needed.

Step 4: Test Before You Commit

Use free trials, demos, or free-tier accounts to test any tool for 7–14 days. During that time, ask:

- Did it save me time?

- Was it easy to learn and use?

- Would I realistically use this every week?

- Is the output something I'd actually share with clients or customers?

If the answer is yes, the tool is worth the investment.

Step 5: Evaluate Return on Investment (ROI)

A $20/month tool may sound expensive—until you realize it saves you 10 hours per month. Always compare **time saved** or **results improved** to the cost.

Evaluate based on:

- Time and effort saved

- Quality of output

- Ease of scaling the task

- Integration with your workflow

Step 6: Review Integration and Automation Options

The best tools are even better when they connect with your existing systems. Look for tools that integrate with:

- Email (Gmail, Outlook)

- Calendar (Google, Office 365)

- CRMs (HubSpot, Zoho, etc.)

- Web forms (Tally, Typeform)

- Project management tools (Notion, Trello, ClickUp)

Suggested Tools by Business Task (As of April 2025)

Task	Tool	Free Version	Paid Plan
Writing emails & blogs	ChatGPT, Jasper	Yes	From $20/month
Creating graphics	Canva AI, Adobe Firefly	Yes	From $12.99/month
Social media scheduling	Buffer, Ocoya	Yes	From $19/month
Workflow automation	Zapier, Make	Yes	From $9/month
Transcribing meetings	Fireflies.ai, Otter.ai	Yes	From $10/month
Lead capture & forms	Tally.so, Typeform	Yes	From $0 to $29/month

Summary

The right AI tool is the one that solves *your* problem, works with *your* systems, and fits *your* budget. Avoid chasing trends. Focus on results. Start small, test thoroughly, and build a stack of tools that support how you work best.

Next, we'll move from selection to implementation: how to **automate repetitive tasks** using AI without technical complexity.

CHAPTER 5

•————————————————•

AUTOMATING YOUR DAILY GRIND WITH AI

Introduction

One of AI's biggest strengths is the ability to take tedious, repetitive tasks off your hands—and do them faster, more consistently, and around the clock.

This chapter shows you how to turn common business tasks into simple, automated workflows. With the right setup, you can reclaim hours each week and reduce the risk of human error—without needing to code or hire a developer.

What AI-Powered Automation Can Handle

- Send automatic emails after a form submission

- Generate custom thank-you or follow-up messages

- Schedule appointments and send reminders

- Transcribe and summarize meetings

- Automatically moving data between platforms (e.g., leads into a spreadsheet)

These aren't just time savers. They're consistently builders—ensuring that no lead goes uncontacted, and no task falls through the cracks.

What to Automate First

Start with tasks that are:

- Repetitive

- Time-consuming

- Low risk

- Often delayed or forgotten

Examples:

- Welcome emails

- Post-meeting follow-ups

- Monthly report generation

- Social media scheduling

Sample Automation: Lead Follow-Up

Workflow:

1. A new lead submits a form on your website.

2. Zapier picks up the form submission.

3. ChatGPT generates a personalized follow-up email.

4. Gmail sends the email automatically.

5. The lead's info is logged in a spreadsheet or CRM.

Time saved: 10–15 minutes per lead

Consistency improved: 100%

Recommended Tools for Automation

Tool	Use Case	Free Version	Paid Plan
Zapier	Connect apps and trigger actions	Yes	From $0 to $49/month
Make	Visual automation builder	Yes	From $9/month
Calendly	Schedule meetings and reminders	Yes	From $10/month
Fireflies.ai	Transcribe and summarize meetings	Yes	From $10/month
Tally.so	Lead capture and workflows	Yes	From $0 to $29/month

Tips for Effective Automation

- **Document your workflows.** This helps you refine and update over time.

- **Start small.** Automate one task and measure its impact before expanding.

- **Test regularly.** Even automated systems need monitoring.

- **Don't automate everything.** Keep a human touch where empathy matters.

Summary

Automation is not about doing less. It's about doing *more of what matters* by handing off routine work to systems that don't forget, don't slow down, and don't make careless mistakes.

In the next chapter, you'll learn how to apply AI to one of your most critical business functions: **marketing**.

CHAPTER 6

•————————————————•

MARKETING MADE EASIER WITH AI

Introduction

Marketing is a major challenge for most small business owners—not because you don't know it's important, but because it takes time, creativity, and consistency.

AI changes that. With the right tools, you can generate content, visuals, emails, ads, and insights—quickly and affordably. This chapter gives you a complete overview of how AI can enhance every area of your marketing efforts.

AI for Content Creation

Content is the foundation of digital marketing. AI can help you:

- Write blog posts

- Generate social media captions

- Draft email newsletters

- Personalize customer messages

Tools like **ChatGPT**, **Jasper**, and **Copy.ai** can generate content in your brand's tone, saving hours each week.

AI for Design and Branding

You no longer need a designer for every post or campaign.

With tools like **Canva AI** and **Adobe Firefly**, you can:

- Create branded visuals quickly

- Resize designs for multiple platforms

- Generate custom images or templates

- Maintain brand consistency across all channels

AI for Email Marketing

Email is still one of the highest-ROI marketing tools. AI helps by:

- Writing subject lines and body copy

- Segmenting your audience

- Timing your campaigns for better opening rates

- Personalizing content automatically

Platforms like **MailerLite**, **Brevo**, and **Seventh Sense** offer built-in AI features.

AI for Social Media

You can use AI to:

- Write and schedule posts

- Suggest trending hashtags

- Analyze what type of content performs best

Tools like **Ocoya**, **Buffer**, and **Lately.ai** combine writing, planning, and posting into a single dashboard.

AI for Paid Advertising

Running ads? AI can:

- Generate variations of copy and visuals

- Test multiple headlines or CTAs

- Optimize spending based on real-time performance

Platforms like **AdCreative.ai** or **Copy.ai** help speed up campaign creation.

Sample Weekly AI Marketing Workflow

Monday: Use ChatGPT to write a blog post
Tuesday: Repurpose blog into social posts with Ocoya
Wednesday: Use Canva AI to design visual content
Thursday: Schedule posts and emails using Buffer
Friday: Review performance data and adjust

Summary

AI takes the heavy lifting out of marketing. It helps you stay visible, sound professional, and create consistent content without needing a big budget or team. When used properly, AI becomes your marketing assistant—always ready to write, design, analyze, and optimize.

CHAPTER 7

STAYING HUMAN IN AN AI WORLD

Introduction

AI can do a lot. It can write, design, schedule, and analyze. But there's one thing it can't do—and that's replace your **human presence**, **empathy**, and **relationship with customers**.

As more businesses adopt AI tools, standing out won't just be about how efficient you are. It will be about how **real** you feel.

This chapter shows how to use AI without losing the personality, voice, and values that make your business unique.

Why Human Connection Still Matters

Even with AI doing part of the work, your customers still want:

- Real connection

- Personalized communication

- Authentic values and voice

- Honest responses

- Emotional intelligence

In the world of smart machines, being human becomes a strategic advantage.

Where AI Falls Short

AI is fast, consistent, and scalable—but it lacks:

- Emotional awareness

- Moral reasoning

- Cultural context

- Intuition

Which means it can misunderstand tone, offer robotic replies, or make awkward mistakes. That's why **you remain the most important part** of your business—even when you use AI extensively.

How to Stay Human While Using AI

1. Define and Preserve Your Brand Voice

Before using AI to create content, define your tone:

- Are you formal or casual?

- Warm or authoritative?

- Friendly or witty?

Feed that tone into your AI tools using prompt instructions, templates, or examples. Always review and lightly edit AI-generated content to match your style.

2. Personalize Your Communication

Even if AI drafts your emails or messages:

- Include real names

- Reference specific events or conversations

- Add personal touches (a short thank you, a sign-off, a custom sentence)

AI can't care—but you can.

3. Keep Sensitive Communication Human

Avoid automating:

- Responses to complaints

- Refund or billing issues

- Emotional conversations

- Complex negotiations

These require judgment, empathy, and understanding skills only humans have.

4. Be Transparent About Use of AI (When Relevant)

Customers don't need to know every detail of your tech stack—but it helps to be transparent when it matters.

You might say:

- "This message was generated using smart tools and reviewed by our team."

- "This confirmation was sent by our automation system, but we're here if you need anything."

Transparency builds trust—especially when it's paired with responsiveness.

Ethical Use of AI in Small Business

AI also raises important ethical questions:

- Are you using AI responsibly?

- Is the customer data you use protected?

- Are you crediting sources or disclosing automated content?

As a business owner, your responsibility is to:

- Use only trusted tools with clear privacy policies

- Avoid using AI to mislead or impersonate

- Maintain oversight of all automated communication

Ethics isn't about complexity, it's about **honesty, respect, and consent**.

Real Examples of Staying Human with AI

Example 1:

An online coach uses ChatGPT to write newsletters—but always adds a personal note at the top and invites replies.

Example 2:

A local store automates follow-ups—but records a short welcome video for each new customer.

Example 3:

A digital agency uses AI to draft social content—but only posts what a human has reviewed, refined, and approved.

These businesses use AI to scale **efficiency**—not to replace **authenticity**.

Summary

AI can multiply your productivity. But only you can multiply your relationships. By blending smart tools with your human intuition, voice, and presence, you create a business that feels both modern and meaningful.

In the final chapter, we'll look ahead—at how to **future-proof your business** in a world where AI will only become more powerful and more common.

CHAPTER 8

FUTURE-PROOFING YOUR BUSINESS WITH AI

Introduction

A I isn't a trend. It's a foundational shift in how businesses operate. And it's moving fast—new tools, models, and use cases emerge every month.

But here's the good news: You don't have to chase every change. Future proofing isn't about knowing everything. It's about building a mindset, systems, and habits that help you adapt to *anything*.

This chapter shows you how to stay ahead of the curve—without losing focus or burning out.

What Future Proofing Actually Means

To future-proof your business in the future, you need three things:

1. **Curiosity** — Stay open to learning

2. **Flexibility** — Be ready to adapt workflows and tools

3. **Clarity** — Know your goals and filter out distractions

Businesses that stay rigid will struggle. Those that stay curious and adaptive will thrive.

How to Stay Current Without Overwhelm

You don't need to follow everything, just **follow the right things consistently**.

Step 1: Subscribe to One or Two Trusted AI Newsletters

These summarize tool updates, trends, and new use cases.

Recommended (as of April 2025):

- Ben's Bites

- The Rundown AI

- TLDR AI

- FutureTools Weekly

- Chain of Thought (Zain Kahn)

Set aside **10 minutes a week** to scan headlines and explore anything relevant.

Step 2: Test New Tools with a Purpose

Don't test every new app. Instead, ask:

- "Will this tool solve a current business problem?"

- "Can I test it in under an hour?"

- "Does it improve something I'm already doing?"

Try one new tool per month. Keep what works. Discard what doesn't.

Step 3: Build Up Your Prompting Skills

Prompting is the new keyboard. The better your prompts, the better your AI results.

Practice by:

- Giving clearer instructions

- Including tone, format, and length preferences

- Asking for revisions ("make it more concise," "rewrite in a friendly tone")

Prompting is a learnable skill—and it's what separates casual users from confident ones.

Keep Your Systems Flexible

Avoid building rigid, locked-in systems. Instead:

- Use modular tools (Zapier, Notion, Airtable)

- Document your processes

- Schedule time once a quarter to review and improve

Your business doesn't need to be perfect—it just needs to be **ready to evolve**.

Invest in Digital Literacy

AI tools will change, but the skill of learning and applying them will never go out of date.

What to focus on:

- Understanding how tools work (not just how to use them)

- Learning how data flows through your systems

- Following ethical, privacy-conscious best practices

This gives you long-term confidence—no matter what the future holds.

Recommended Tools for Staying Ahead (As of April 2025)

Tool	Use Case	Free Version	Paid Plan
Futurepedia.io	Discover new AI tools	Yes	Free
Toolify.ai	Tool discovery and reviews	Yes	Free
FlowGPT	Prompt marketplace and tutorials	Yes	Free & Paid
Product Hunt	Track new launches (AI category)	Yes	Free
OpenAI Playground	Test GPT-based tools and features	Yes	Pay-as-you-go

Summary

Future-proofing your business with AI means building a system that can flex, grow, and adapt—not chasing every new trend, but having the clarity to know which tools help you move forward.

AI will continue to change—but your ability to **learn, lead, and connect with your customers** will always be your strongest asset.

APPENDICES

Appendix A

AI Terms Glossary

Artificial Intelligence (AI)

Technology that enables machines or software to simulate human-like intelligence, such as understanding language, recognizing patterns, or making decisions.

Machine Learning (ML)

A method by which AI systems learn and improve over time through data, rather than being explicitly programmed.

Natural Language Processing (NLP)

A branch of AI that enables software to understand, interpret, and respond to human language.

Large Language Model (LLM)

An AI model trained on enormous amounts of text data to generate human-like responses. ChatGPT is a type of LLM.

Generative AI

A category of AI that can create new content—text, images, video, or audio—rather than just analyzing existing data.

Prompt

The input or instruction a user gives an AI system in order to generate a response.

Automation

Using software to complete repetitive tasks with little or no human input.

API (Application Programming Interface)

A set of tools that allow different software applications to connect and exchange data.

No-Code / Low-Code

Tools that allow non-programmers to create workflows, websites, and automations without needing to write software code.

Training Data

The data used to "teach" an AI model how to perform a task— such as recognizing speech or generating responses.

Appendix B

AI Starter Kits by Business Type

These toolkits are suggestions for small business owners based on common needs. You can mix and match, depending on your business model.

Service-Based Businesses (e.g., Coaching, Consulting, Freelancing)

Key Needs: Client communication, content creation, lead management

Task	Recommended Tool
Email and proposal writing	ChatGPT, Jasper
Scheduling and reminders	Calendly, Zapier
Content marketing	Canva AI, Jasper
Meeting notes	Fireflies.ai, Otter.ai
Testimonials and feedback	Tally.so, Typeform

Product-Based Businesses (e.g., eCommerce, Retail)

Key Needs: Product listings, marketing content, visuals, customer support

Task	Recommended Tool
Product descriptions	Copy.ai, ChatGPT
Visual ads and branding	Canva AI, AdCreative.ai
Social media management	Ocoya, Buffer
Customer chat & automation	Tidio AI, Manychat

Task	Recommended Tool
SEO blog content	Jasper, Surfer SEO

Local or In-Person Businesses (e.g., Clinics, Wellness, Trades)

Key Needs: Scheduling, follow-up, client engagement

Task	Recommended Tool
Appointment scheduling	Calendly, TidyCal
Customer onboarding emails	MailerLite, Brevo
Social media posts	Canva, Ocoya
Review requests and tracking	Google Forms, ChatGPT

Appendix C

Smart Prompting Tips

The quality of AI output depends on the quality of your input. The better your prompt, the better your result.

Prompting Formula:

Goal + Context + Tone + Format + Constraints

Example Prompt:

"Write a friendly welcome email for a new client who has booked a 1:1 session. Keep it under 150 words, in a conversational but professional tone."

Tips for Better Prompts

- **Be specific.** Tell the AI what you want, who it's for, and what tone to use.

- **Add examples.** Say, "Use a tone similar to this: [insert example]."

- **Give structure.** Ask for bullet points, numbered lists, or specific formatting.

- **Refine.** Use follow-ups like "Make it shorter" or "Add a stronger call to action."

Prompt Templates

- "Write a 3-paragraph blog post about [topic] for [audience]. Tone: casual but informative."

- "List 5 headline ideas for a newsletter about [product or event]."

- "Summarize this article for LinkedIn in under 100 words. Add hashtags."

- "Rewrite this message to sound more confident and persuasive."

- "Draft a follow-up email for a lead who hasn't responded in 3 days."

Appendix D

AI Tool Evaluation Checklist

Before committing to any AI tool, evaluate it using this checklist.

Usefulness

- Does it solve a current business problem?

- Will I use it regularly?

Ease of Use

- Is the interface simple to learn?

- Are there tutorials or templates?

Value for Cost

- Does it save time or increase output?

- Does the price align with the value it provides?

Integration

- Does it work with tools I already use?

- Can it automate part of my workflow?

Support & Stability

- Is the company reputable and well-reviewed?

- Is there customer support if something goes wrong?

Appendix E

Resources for Continued Learning

Courses and Training

- **Coursera – AI for Everyone (Andrew Ng)**

- **Google Digital Garage – Machine Learning Basics**

- **LinkedIn Learning – AI in Small Business**

- **HubSpot Academy – Marketing Automation and AI**

Directories and Communities

- **FutureTools.io** – Directory of AI tools by category

- **Product Hunt (AI tag)** – New AI products daily

- **FlowGPT** – Prompt sharing community

- **Reddit – r/SmallBusiness** – Peer advice and use cases

- **Indie Hackers** – Tools and success stories

Recommended Newsletters

These are great for staying up to date in under 10 minutes a week.

- **Ben's Bites** – Daily roundup of AI news and tools

- **The Rundown AI** – Weekly summaries and tutorials

- **FutureTools Weekly** – Curated tool picks

- **TLDR AI** – Concise, no-fluff updates

- **Chain of Thought (Zain Kahn)** – Strategic trends and business analysis

FINAL NOTES

AI isn't a trend, it's a transformation. But it's also just a tool. It only becomes powerful when paired with clarity, intention, and action.

Start where you are. Don't worry about doing everything perfectly. Test one tool. Automate one task. Delegate one chunk of work to an AI assistant.

Build smarter systems that help you:

- Reclaim time

- Reduce burnout

- Improve service

- Create consistency

- Scale with less stress

This book is just the beginning. Your business is the real engine of innovation.

FINAL CONCLUSION

Smarter Business, Human Results

You've made it to the end of this guide—and that already sets you apart.

Most people *talk* about embracing new tools. You've now taken the time to **understand how AI works**, where it fits in your business, and how to begin using it in a practical, non-technical way.

This book wasn't about becoming a programmer, data scientist, or futurist. It was about giving you the tools, knowledge, and confidence to:

- **Save time**

- **Market more consistently**

- **Deliver better customer experiences**

- **Work more efficiently**

- **Grow with less stress**

Let's recap what we've covered:

- **Chapter 1** gave you a clear, grounded understanding of AI—no hype, no confusion

- **Chapter 2** explained why AI is a serious opportunity for small business owners today

- **Chapter 3** walked you through the basic components of how AI systems work

- **Chapter 4** taught you how to choose the right tools (and avoid the wrong ones)

- **Chapter 5** showed how automation can free you from daily grind tasks

- **Chapter 6** helped you scale your marketing with minimal effort

- **Chapter 7** focused on keeping your brand voice and values front and center

- **Chapter 8** showed how to future-proof your business—no matter what comes next

You Don't Need to Master Everything

You just need to:

- Pick **one area** where AI can help you today

- Test **one tool**

- Automate **one task**

- Write **one prompt**

- Start **one smarter habit**

AI won't replace you. But it will **reward** you for being flexible, curious, and action oriented.

This is not about perfection, it's about **progress**.

FINAL THOUGHT

In business, the ones who thrive aren't always the biggest, fastest, or loudest. They're the ones who adapt, evolve, and **stay connected to what really matters**.

If you combine AI's speed with your vision, voice, and humanity, you're not just running a smarter business.
You're building a stronger one.

So take what you've learned, apply it with intention, and keep going.

Your next breakthrough might be **one tool**, **one idea**, or **one prompt** away.

Let AI handle the systems.

You keep leading the business.

ABOUT THE AUTHOR

Mohamed Mawji is a seasoned entrepreneur and technology innovator whose career has shaped the business and tech landscapes for nearly half a century. Launching his first venture at just nineteen, he entered the emerging technology scene before the rise of IBM and Microsoft—quickly established himself at the forefront of a rapidly evolving industry.

Beginning as a print broker, Mawji went on to establish an award-winning clone system builder in the 1980s, which made a significant mark by introducing one of the first removable hard disk solutions—an innovation ahead of its time.

His journey is defined by resilience and adaptability. Through economic downturns and shifting markets, Mawji repeatedly demonstrated his ability to launch, scale, and lead companies through complex challenges. Before retiring in 2022, he served as CEO of a NAS systems integration firm, reaffirming his relevance and innovation in a dynamic industry.

In parallel with his business ventures, Mawji remained committed to lifelong learning, earning a BA in 2009 and an MBA in 2019, strengthening the academic foundation behind his practical experience.

He is also the author of several well-regarded books on business, sales, recovery, and innovation, including:

- *The New Business Blueprint: A Step-by-Step Guide for Startup Success*

- *Beyond Solutions: Mastering Outcomes for Sales Supremacy*

- *Rising from the Ashes: A Complete Guide to Recovering from Business Failure*

- *Synthetica: Orchestrating the Future with Artificial Intelligence, Big Data, and Robotics*

- *NEURISE - Elevating Minds with Ai*

- *AI for Small Business Owners: A Practical Guide to Automating, Marketing, and Growing Smarter with Artificial Intelligence*

His legacy continues to inspire a new generation of entrepreneurs, technologists, and forward-thinkers seeking to shape the future.